Foxton Primary SCIENCE

Carnivores
Herbivores
Omnivores

First published 2019
Foxton Books
London, UK

Copyright © Foxton Books, 2019

ISBN: 978-1-911481-95-9

Written by Nichola Tyrrell
Designed by Maryke Goldie
Logo design: Stewart Wright (2Wright Design)
Cover design: Ed White
Education consultant: Frances Barlow

About Foxton Primary Science:

The Foxton Primary Science series supports **Key Stage 1** Science through a variety of features and **STEAM**-inspired tasks that cover all curriculum requirements.

Colourful, engaging content blends information with prompts for further discussion and investigation.

Keywords, creative activities and quizzes reinforce comprehension, along with challenging words (in bold) explained in the glossary.

Contents

What do animals eat?

Like humans, animals need to eat food to stay alive, to grow and for **energy**. We can group animals together by the type of food they eat.

tiger

Carnivores are animals that catch and eat the flesh, or meat, of other animals.

Keywords carnivore herbivore omnivore

Herbivores are animals that eat only plants.

panda

Which group (or groups) do humans belong to? Are you a carnivore, herbivore or omnivore?

Omnivores are animals that eat both plants and meat.

badger

Body structure and diet

Animals eat food that suits their body **structure**. Many animals have a stomach and teeth that are built for eating plants or meat or both.

crocodile

Carnivores have sharp pointy teeth for tearing animal **flesh**. They also have excellent senses to smell, watch and hear their prey.

Keywords digest predator senses

Plants can be hard to digest. Herbivores have a stomach that digests plants easily. They also have flat teeth that crush and grind plants into tiny pieces.

rabbit

squirrel

Omnivores like the squirrel have a **combination** of these features to eat both plants and animals.

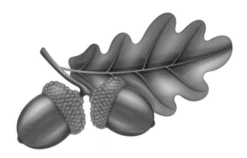

Make a Venn diagram of the following animals. Draw two circles that overlap: one for carnivores and one for herbivores. The space in the middle is for the omnivores.

- elephant
- deer
- monkey
- wolf
- fox
- lion

Carnivores: mammals

Mammals are hairy, **warm-blooded** animals with either four legs or no legs at all. Most give birth to live young. Carnivorous mammals include the dog and cat families, racoons, seals and sea lions.

In a pride of lions, it is the females who do most of the hunting for prey.

buffalo

female lion

Keywords carnivorous mammal prey

wolf

sea lion

Like all carnivores, wolves have powerful jaws and teeth.

Sea lions are carnivorous mammals that feed only on fish, squid and octopus.

Draw a picture of your favourite carnivorous mammal.

Dogs and cats are carnivores too.

Carnivores: reptiles, amphibians and fish

Most reptiles, amphibians and fish are carnivores. Many are able to eat animals much larger than themselves! All must hunt carefully to get their next meal.

Snakes are reptiles that swallow food whole as they do not have teeth built for chewing.

This green snake can open its jaws wide enough to swallow a lizard!

Keywords   amphibian   fish   reptile

bullfrog

An African bullfrog prepares to enjoy an unsuspecting grasshopper!

Engineer a new carnivore. It could be a mammal, a reptile or any other type of animal. Think about what it needs to catch and eat other creatures: type of teeth or tongue, strong senses, claws? Draw your new carnivore or make a figure with modelling clay.

This great white shark is chasing a seal for its next meal.

great white shark

alligator

A fish is no match for an alligator!

Carnivores: birds and minibeasts

With their **ability** to fly, birds can hunt their prey from far away. Little minibeasts have other skills to catch prey, such as weaving a web or giving a venomous sting!

Many birds, like the osprey, can catch fish near the water's surface while flying.

eagle

Keywords bird invertebrate minibeast venomous

spider

butterfly

Spiders trap food in their sticky webs.

This hungry heron is stalking fish in a **marsh**.

heron

ants

Some carnivorous ants use venomous stingers to catch their prey.

Make a carnivore collage. Research online and print out pictures of carnivores from different animal groups. Glue them on card to make a collage.

Herbivores: mammals

Some of the biggest mammals in the world eat only plants. They get their **nutrients** from leaves, roots, grasses, fruits, vegetables and bulbs.

elephant

Elephants use their powerful trunks to grab tasty leaves.

Keywords domesticated vegetation wild

In the wild, horses eat only grass. **Domesticated** horses are also fed bran, oats, barley and hay. A horse's teeth are flat, not pointed. This helps it to grind down grass and other dry vegetation.

wild horses

flat teeth

Do you know of three more herbivorous mammals? How could you find out?

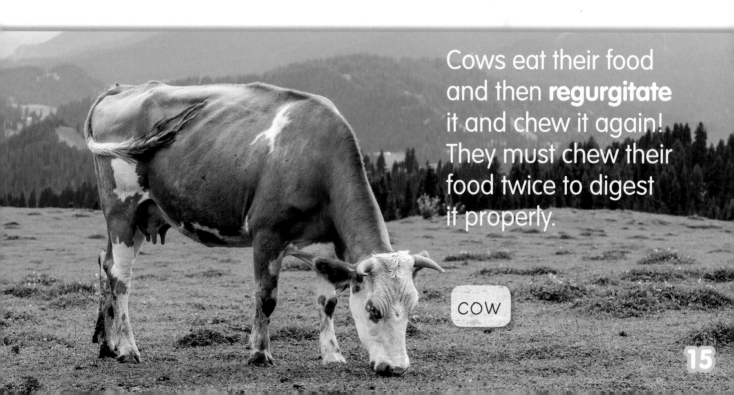

Cows eat their food and then **regurgitate** it and chew it again! They must chew their food twice to digest it properly.

cow

Herbivores: reptiles, amphibians and fish

Many fish eat only **aquatic** plants. Most amphibians and reptiles are carnivores but there are a few that eat only **vegetation**.

Iguanas are reptiles that not only eat leaves and fruit but flowers too!

iguana

Keywords   algae   coral   iguana   tadpole

Amphibian tadpoles are herbivorous until they reach **adulthood** and become carnivorous frogs.

Tropical parrotfish get their name from their beak-like snouts which they use to scrape algae off of coral.

Crack the code to find out the name for humans who eat only plants.

Complete each sum, then write the word using the letter code below for each answer:

9 + 4 = _____

17 - 12 = _____

21 - 13 = _____

4 + 5 = _____

3 x 5 = _____

Try writing your own code cracker to challenge your friends!

Letter code:

8 = g   5 = e

9 = a   13 = v

15 = n

Herbivores: birds and minibeasts

Plant-eating birds and minibeasts eat more than just leaves. Some nibble on tree bark and buds, flowers, seeds and other plant parts.

swans

Few birds are total herbivores although large waterfowl, such as swans, eat mostly aquatic plants.

Keywords   insect   minibeast   waterfowl

Many insects, snails, slugs, mites, millipedes, and worms are minibeast herbivores.

Aphids suck the juices out of plant leaves, stems and roots.

Caterpillars chomp on leaves.

Honey bees collect pollen and nectar from flowers.

Make a bar chart that shows the smallest and the biggest herbivores you can think of. Compare their sizes. How do they eat?

Omnivores: mammals

Omnivorous mammals have both sharp pointy canine teeth for chewing meat and flat molar teeth for grinding plants. These animals have the biggest choice of food.

Farm pigs are fed mostly soybean meal and corn, but in the wild they **forage** for all sorts of plants plus insects and even fish.

pig

Keywords choice forage mammal

monkey

This monkey loves its oranges! Monkeys might also eat seeds, flowers, birds' eggs and some minibeasts.

Play animal charades with your friends and guess the animal and whether it is a carnivore, herbivore or omnivore. Players take turns acting out the movements of an animal and how it eats.

rat

Rats will eat just about anything, including leftover human food if they get the chance!

Omnivores: reptiles, amphibians and fish

Omnivorous reptiles include many species of lizard and turtle. There are plenty of fish in this group too, but no known omnivorous amphibians.

chameleon

This hungry chameleon is stretching out its long sticky tongue to catch a cricket.

Keywords chameleon piranha tortoise

A slow-moving snail is easy prey for a tortoise!

snail

tortoise

What am I?
Play this game with your friends. Each player chooses an animal and finds out five facts about it. Write down your facts and players then take turns reading aloud one fact while the others try to guess the animal being described.

While the piranha fish does eat plants, its sharp teeth are well-built for tearing flesh too!

piranha

Omnivores: birds and minibeasts

Some omnivores eat different foods at different stages of their lives. Many baby animals need meat-based foods for growth and then eat more plants when they are fully grown.

robin

A mother robin brings a juicy worm to feed her babies. When they are older, the young will eat seeds and berries.

Keywords bluejay   robin   stink bug

This bluejay is **skilled** at eating while upside down – sometimes that is the only way to grab those seeds!

Make an animal food group poster.

Choose two animals for each of the three groups: carnivore, herbivore, omnivore. Draw the animals in the correct group and list the foods they eat.

bluejay

stink bug

Stink bugs (or shield bugs) get their name from the smelly odour they produce when under attack from predators. They use their mouthparts to **pierce** plants and other insects and suck the juices inside.

25

Food chains

All animals and plants need food to stay alive. They are all part of a food chain. A food chain shows how animals and plants need each other to survive.

A herbivore such as the vole eats grass.

vole

Keywords   alive   food chain   survive

A carnivore like the owl eats the vole.

owl

The omnivorous fox eats both the vole and the owl!

fox

There are lots of different food chains. Can you think of a forest food chain?

Make a 3-D food chain scene that includes animals from each group.

- Think about where to place the animals depending on whether they are a carnivore, omnivore or herbivore.
- Collect things from outside to set your scene, such as moss, stones, twigs and leaves.

Comprehension check

Choose the correct answer from options a–c.

1. Herbivores eat only:
   a) animals   b) plants   c) both

2. An animal that eats only meat is:
   a) an omnivore   b) a carnivore c) a herbivore

3. Which of these animals is a herbivore?
   a) elephant   b) snake   c) squirrel

4. Aphids suck juice from plants. They are:
   a) carnivores   b) herbivores c) omnivores

5. Which animal eats only plants?
   a) badger   b) panda   c) monkey

6. What type of chain do all animals and plants belong to?
   a) food   b) key   c) gold

7. There are no known omnivores of which animal group?
   a) reptiles   b) fish   c) amphibians

8. Which animals have mostly sharp pointy teeth?
   a) carnivores   b) herbivores c) omnivores

Turn to page 32 to mark your answers.

Vocabulary check

Fill in the blanks to complete these animal facts:

1. An animal that eats meat and plants is
   an _ _ _ _ _ _ _ _ _ .

2. Carnivores eat animal f _ _ _ _ .

3. An animal that eats only plants is
   a _ _ _ _ _ _ _ _ _ _ .

4. Herbivores have a d _ _ _ _ _ _ _ _ _ system that
   can process plants easily.

5. Carnivores have sharp _ _ _ _ _ for tearing flesh.

6. A food _ _ _ _ _ shows how animals and plants
   need each other to survive.

7. Cows r _ _ _ _ _ _ _ _ _ _ _ their food and
   chew it again.

8. A baby frog is a t _ _ _ _ _ _ .

9. An animal that hunts other animals is
   a p _ _ _ _ _ _ _ .

10. An animal that is hunted by other animals
    is p _ _ _ .

Turn to page 32 to mark your answers.

How do insects eat?

Some insects have mouthparts that can chew food. But many insects, like aphids and butterflies, have a straw-like proboscis and cannot chew. How do they eat?

You will need:
- 1 drinking straw
- 1 small cup of water
- 1 small cup of cereal (that is too big to fit in the straw)

Now pretend to be a butterfly that needs some food!
1. Hold one end of the straw in your mouth (your proboscis) and keep your hands at your sides.
2. Try to suck up the cereal with the straw.
3. Then, try to suck up some of the water (the nectar of a flower).

What happened when you tried to eat the cereal with the straw?

What happened with the water?

Why do you think butterflies only feed on liquids?

Glossary

ability – the quality of being able; the power to do something

adulthood – the time of life when a person is grown up

aquatic – in water

combination – two or more things that are brought together

energy – in animals, the power or ability to be active

engineer – to design and build something

flesh – the part of an animal used as food; soft tissue between skin and bones

forage – to search

pierce – to make a hole

regurgitate – to bring up food that has been eaten, from the stomach

skilled – to be good at doing a task

structure – the way in which parts are joined together to form something, such as parts of an animal's body

vegetation – plants or plant life

warm-blooded – an animal whose body temperature stays the same even if it is very cold outside

Index

Quiz answers

Comprehension check, page 28

1. b, 2. b, 3. a, 4. b, 5. b, 6. a, 7. c, 8. a

Vocabulary check, page 29

1. omnivore, 2. flesh, 3. herbivore, 4. digestive, 5. teeth,
6. chain, 7. regurgitate, 8. tadpole, 9. predator, 10. prey

Photo credits

Shutterstock.com: cover: JaklZdenek; pp 1–2: GraphicsRF, arbit; pp 4–5: Chepko Danil Vitalevich, Khoroshunova Olga, Michal Ninger, graphic-line; pp 6–7: Somluck Rungaree, Paul Reeves Photography, Vinnikava Viktoryia, vixenkristy; pp 8–9: Maggy Meyer, Michal Ninger, Santiparp Wattanaporn, Chendongshan, MOSAIC; pp 10–11: tsnebula23, Milan Zygmunt, Sergey Uryadnikov, John Cawthron, zenstock; pp 12–13: Monty Cob, EarthArts Photography, H. Evan Miller, Stacey Ann Alberts, ALEXEY GRIGOREV, Lorelyn Medina; pp 14–15: Michael Potter11, JoffreyM, 06photo, ivandan; pp 16–17: Don Mammoser, Savo Ilic, Pavaphon Supanantananont, Ellagrin; pp 18–19: Sergei25, Simeon Kolev, Sunti, Floki, GraphicsRF; pp 20–21: Simun Ascic, The Perfect, torook, KVanHorn; pp 22–23: Cathy Keifer, Dave Montreuil, Grigorii Pisotsckii; pp 24–25: Tony Campbell, Alexander Sviridov, Radu Bercan; pp 26–27: M Rose, Miroslav Hlavko, Karin Jaehne, PinkPeng, brgfx; pp 28–29: arbit; pp :30–32: BlueRingMedia, mukmin007, NEGOVURA, Mariyana M, Lorelyn Medina, Birdydiz